TO: _____

FROM:_____

Life needs portals to express itself through:
a plant, an animal or a person. The seed of your
future success already lives within you.
Discover how much more successful
you can be. ~ Jim Cathcart

Copyright © 2024 Jim Cathcart

Jim Cathcart ~ Mini Book of Quotes

All rights reserved. No part of this publication may be reproduced, distributed, or transmitted in any form or by any means, including photocopying, recording, or other electronic or mechanical methods, without the prior written permission of the publisher, except in the case of brief quotations embodied in critical reviews and certain other noncommercial uses permitted by copyright law. For permission requests, write to the publisher, addressed "Attention: Permissions Coordinator," at info@beyondpublishing.net

Quantity sales and special discounts are available on quantity purchases by corporations, associations, and others. For details, contact the publisher at the address above.

Orders by U.S. trade bookstores and wholesalers. Email info@ BeyondPublishing.net

The Beyond Publishing Speakers Bureau can bring authors to your live event. For more information or to book an event contact the Beyond Publishing Speakers Bureau speak@BeyondPublishing.net

The Author can be reached directly at BeyondPublishing.net

Manufactured and printed in the United States of America distributed globally by BeyondPublishing.net

New York | Los Angeles | London | Sydney

ISBN Softcover:

Jim Cathcart is one of the best known and most award-winning motivational speakers in the business. It was his passion and his purpose that motivated him to pursue his dream of becoming a motivational speaker and trainer inspiring others to grow to their full potential ~ like the acorn that becomes the mighty oak! His personal purpose statement which he carries with him is:

"Through Intelligent Observation, Vocal Appreciation and Full Self Expression I inspire myself and others to Live More Abundantly."

Jim's life and career have been an expression of that purpose, as seen in his 27 published books, 3,500 convention speeches, millions of TEDx viewers, Awards, Honors, Leadership Positions, and a career of enduring friendships with clients and colleagues around the world.

MOTIVATION, STRATEGY, TRAINING

MINI BOOK OF
QUOTES

This book is a collection of quotes and thoughts from Jim Cathcart as expressed through all of his works and his public appearances. We recommend that you refer to it often, just pick a random quote and focus your attention on what that idea could mean to you. Share the quotes with others, put your favorites in places where you will see them often.

Together in the Spirit of Growth we can not only make our own lives better, but we can make the world better for everyone.

PERSONAL GROWTH & DEVELOPMENT:

How would the person I'd like to be do the things I'm about to do?

An acorn that only thinks as an acorn will never become a mighty oak!

Stem – your past, connection to your heritage.

Cap – your present, mentors, teachers, coaches, parents, role models.

Seed – your future, potential, and the legacy you will pass along!

- Know your nature.
- Explore your nature.
- Nurture your nature.

Nature teaches us if we listen.

What seed of potential sleeps within you?

Grow roots to seek resources and branches to seek opportunities.

Self-Awareness: If you don't know You, you won't understand others.

Mindset: The way you Think will select the Actions you take. Mind your thoughts with care.

Mindset: Scarcity or Abundance? Fixed or Growth? Take or Give? Choose well.

Habit: Your repeated Actions become your Habits. Each action matters.

Reputation: Your Habits determine how you are known.

Opening Doors: Your Reputation determines who will be eager to see you, & who will avoid you.

Growth: Acorns can't become Giant Redwoods, but they are The Best at being Oaks.

Honorable: Years from now your descendants will talk about their heritage. Make them proud.

Accountable: The truth is always there, make sure you see it while it is fresh and new.

MOTIVATION:

Motive + Action = Motivation.

Become the Person who will Attract what you Want.
Be a Magnet.

The world needs what you can give.
Live abundantly and generously.

Gratitude is a spiritual magnet.
It attracts more of what you appreciate.

Maturity is the ability to do what needs to be done
when you don't feel like doing it yet.

If you want to have great success,
first you must become a great person.

Life is about Knowing and Doing,
Both are within your control.

Thoughts are Things. Watch your thoughts with care.

Growth and Joy are only achieved
when you are willing to be uncomfortable.

Show people reasons to believe in themselves.

Help People Live More Abundantly.

How do you motivate people or yourself? What people want is what causes them to take action. Connect with that, and motivation is more straightforward.

Don't seek to feel better, instead seek to become better.

Optimism is a matter of mind not just a matter of might.

If you are not ready for it, then it won't be "your" opportunity.

You can grow through difficulties, but only if you always look for a better way.

Habits are actions you have embraced and repeated. They have no power until you give it to them.

Make time for what you love. Joy is necessary for an abundant life. You get better when you live fully.

LEADERSHIP

Leadership is the ability to get others to WANT to do what needs to be done.

The Future You See Reveals The Person You Will Need To Be.

Great leaders care about their people, and people want to follow them.

A Team is a group of people committed to a common goal.

Every organization has a DNA, a genetic code. It is found in the Vision, Values and Beliefs of its people.

Don't just work; enjoy the work, people, and places where you do it. Make every part of your life reflect the person you want to be.

Get Ready! The more you are ready for, the more options you will have when things change again.

Become the person who would achieve your goals.

You are always leading by example.

Be a magnet for the success you seek.

If you want to be admired, look for things to admire about others.

Be a magnet for the life you want, be an "eligible receiver."

The world treasures Problem Solvers. Be one!

The Causation Chain of Choices: Mindset, Actions, Habits, Reputation, Relationships, Future.

How do you reach the Top 1% of your field?
Study the industry or profession, the best and most respected people in it, and the value it provides to the world, and do likewise.

Commit to improving your profession and being of service as a professional. That will propel you to the top of the field.

Send money ahead to the person you will be 30 years from now. Save and invest. Take time to savor this wonderful life.

See past the process and isolate the purpose. For example: what is the purpose of business? Is it profit? No, profit is an essential by-product of a well-run business. The purpose of the business is to solve a problem or make life better for the customer. Do that, and you'll earn the profits you desire.

SELLING SKILLS:

Sales: The oldest and most profitable Profession.

Make people glad that they know you.

Develop skills you don't need yet.

Yet! Always end a negative with "yet" to hold the door open. "We can't do that…Yet!"

Make life better for people.

What does your buyer really want?

Become the person who will attract the results you seek.

Gratefully asking for help increases your strength.

Recommend others and their gratitude will find its way back to you.

Sales is a form of helping. If you aren't helping, you aren't selling, you are manipulating.

Professional Selling is Problem Solving for Pay.

Anticipate Needs: Think "What if," then find a solution.

Doing a job isn't the same as Doing a job Well.

Money follows value. When you provide value to others, they are inclined to pay you for it.

Money is to a business as blood is to a body. It is not The Purpose of the Business or the Body, but without it, one dies.

Profit is necessary and noble. Without profit you won't be able to continue to serve.

Professionalism: A professional is not merely measured by the business they are in, but by the Way they are in business.

Sales Success: It is not called the "Best Book List", it is called the "Best Sellers List".

Imposter Syndrome: Self-doubt is an Emotional remnant of your former self. Acknowledge it and move on anyway. Others feel it too.

Develop the traits, attitudes, habits, and personal qualities that make others want to hire you or become your friend.

Give people a way to feel or experience the value you can bring. Then they will want to buy.

BUSINESS GROWTH:

Business is the vehicle that a society uses to make its life better. When we feel a need, we create a business.

A business is a living system, an organism, not a mechanism. Like a tree it thrives by attaining the perfect interactive relationship with the ecosystem in which it lives.

Both a business and a tree grow towards opportunity and send out roots to needed resources.

Both a business and tree learn to follow their nature and only their nature through predictable seasons and cycles, shedding unproductive parts and growing new parts as needed.

Both a tree and a business are strengthened by adversity and bear fruit.

Notice more. Grow your awareness (of money, needs, expenses, what's coming, what's working, where are the gaps) Know where you stand.

Give more than you have to. Practice up-serving not just up-selling. (exceed your customers' expectations).

Up-serving is increasing the customer's satisfaction. Up-selling is merely increasing the transaction.

The quickest way to get a raise is to give your customer and your company a raise through your performance.

Grow your profit per sale/account. Provide more value to the customer at an even lower cost to your company. Customers are assets, invest in them constantly.

Grow your ability to deliver value. Increase your possibilities (available credit, experts, investors, colleagues, partners, advisors, connections, and ways to connect.)

Grow your technology. The better your tools, the better your results. Seek resources which can speed or refine your ability to deliver value.

Grow your freedom and flexibility (low inventory of materials, high availability to deliver, high inventory of sales to come) stay financially light on your feet.

Grow your savings and investments. Build a resource you hope you never need.

Grow your existing markets. Do more business with current customers and further penetrate each market.

Grow your image and market presence. Gain more share of mind. Improve and enhance your reputation as a true professional.

Grow your pipeline. Build a large and better reservoir of future customers. Do next year's prospecting now. Identify more qualified buyers.

Grow your inner circle, your closest contacts. Take extra good care of the primary people in your career. They'll become even better resources to you.

Grow your virtual workforce. Find talent that can expand your capabilities without increasing your payroll expenses. Form strategic alliances and connect with expert vendors and colleagues.

Grow new markets. Get outside your usual channels. Ask "who else could benefit from what we do?" Expand your thinking.

Let others sell for you. Grow your referrals. Seek new testimonials and endorsements. Capture examples of how others have benefited from what you do. Make it easy for them to promote you.

Serve your community. Be a responsible citizen. Make the places where you live and work better because you and your business are there.

Grow your industry. Advance the craft in what you do. Join your industry association. Write articles, teach others, support your profession.

Grow your caring, compassion, and sensitivity. Become known as someone who genuinely cares about making a difference. If you don't care about others why should they care about or listen to you?

RELATIONSHIPS:

A Relationship is a Direct Connection between People in which Value is Exchanged.

Relationships: What matters most is Who is Glad that they know You?

Excellent relationships are 100/100 not 50/50. Make a full commitment.

People will teach you how to sell to them if you will pay attention.

Three essentials for a healthy relationship: Mutual Commitment, Open Communication and Clear Expectations.

Sometimes people don't know what they want, so give them suggestions.

If someone won't let go of you, that's not love that is dependency.

Love is caring more about the welfare of the other person than of yourself.

Teach people how you prefer to receive information, details in full or general summary.

Trust is earned. Otherwise, it's just a wager.

To receive more trust, become more trustworthy.

Your Success Team is the 12 or fewer people through whom you produce your results. If one of them left, you'd need to replace them. Who is on your Success Team?

Life is a series of human interactions, and relationships. Treat them as Assets.

DECISION MAKING:

Make a Personal decision and a Practical decision, then choose the best one of the two.

Decisiveness is priceless. Act on your choices. Take initiative.

Ask: What matters most?

Ask: How would the person I'd like to be do what I'm about to do?

Who should make this decision? If not you, then who?

Some decisions should be voted upon, others should be made by one.

When someone asks you a question, ask, "What do they really want to know?"

If you don't know what's possible you will settle for too little. Think bigger.

The number one question is Why? It gives meaning to everything else.

PUBLIC SPEAKING:

The Cathcart Method™ is Jim Cathcart's personal style and approach to public speaking. Jim's style is very natural and thought provoking. His belief is that your greatest strength is found in your natural abilities, not in some magical formula you learned and rehearsed. People tell Jim that his sincerity comes across strongly. They trust him. They can tell that he is telling the truth. This is what we all should seek.

When you cultivate these qualities in yourself you will increase your natural magnetism and your ability to deliver any message with confidence and impact. What has set Jim Cathcart apart as a presenter and caused so many of his mega-successful colleagues to follow his example and hire him to speak to their groups is The Cathcart Method™.

This is not just a skillset; it is a new and more authentic way of being that allows you to be the most powerful person you can be...You!

The formula to do this can be found in a method known as "FIRST PAGE." This is your memory tool for the key elements to this method.

F.I.R.S.T.

F - Flexible – be able to change quickly without losing control

I – Intentional – make everything happen for a reason

R- Real – don't fake it or you won't really make it

S- Sincere – tell the truth, be yourself

T- Thoughtful (and Considerate)

P.A.G.E.

P- Playful – make this fun for everyone

A- Appropriate (and Professional)

G- Grateful – express your appreciation openly

E- Enthusiastic – bring energy, don't expect to receive it from others

The Cathcart Method™: See it done, Think it through, Notice more, Make it you.

The purpose of a speech is to communicate value to the audience.

Value is always determined by the receiver of the value. Find out what they care about.

Prepare both the Message and the Messenger (yourself).

Your state of mind may be more influential than the words you choose to say.

Like, respect and admire every audience. Keep thinking about them till you find reasons to like, respect and admire them. Then tell them what you discovered.

Stories stick. People remember stories more vividly than facts, lists, quotes, illustrations, examples and demonstrations.

Everyone can be a good storyteller. Learn your craft. Be a student of storytelling.

Be sure to stop speaking before they stop listening.

"What this means to you is…" Use this statement often to stay audience focused.

If you use notes, don't try to hide them, just look at them occasionally. If you don't make a big deal of it, they won't either.

Acknowledge distractions but don't dwell on them. "Wow! That was a loud noise." "Face this way to avoid the glare from the windows." "We are 15 minutes from the break so I will move quickly."

GENERAL:

Worry is mentally rehearsing Failure.

When's the last time you gave yourself "a good talking-to"?

How much of the past are you dragging into today? Let it go!

When you pack for a journey, leave the burdens of the past at home.

Want more? Overfill your current space, give more than you must.

Admiration: be specific about what you admire and express it.

Everyone craves acknowledgement. Notice others and share a smile.

Courage is taking action Despite being afraid. Without fear, courage would be impossible.

If you don't struggle you cannot improve. The easy road doesn't lead to success.

Seek difficulty and overcome it. Make effort your goal, not relaxation.

Data when organized is Information. Information when studied reveals Knowledge. Knowledge when applied yields Understanding. Understanding when practiced reveals Wisdom.

The purpose of Filing isn't storage, it is Retrieval. If you filed it and we can't find it, you didn't "file" it, you HID it!

Optimism is the only productive way to think. Find the solution, it exists somewhere.

Pessimism is looking at the limitations and ignoring the possibilities.

The Future you see reveals the Person you'll be. Think bigger.

Through Intelligent Observation, Vocal Appreciation and Full Self Expression I inspire myself and others to live more abundantly.

Nurture your Nature. All acorns become Oaks but only those that commit to growth will become Mighty Oaks that create Forests of Oaks.

Know what you should be curious about. Be Intelligently Curious.

When you Go Pro the rules change for you. A professional operates to higher standards. Professionals look for ways to be more Valuable, Intentional, Disciplined, Accountable and Honorable.

The three power qualities to cultivate are: Clarity, Confidence and Courage.

If you think you can't, think again. You're ignoring your potential.

A Loser is one who gives up. A Failure is an experience, not a state of being. Try again, differently.

A loss does not make a person a loser. Being a loser is a self-inflicted state of mind.

When you make a sale, immediately initiate another sales call.

Call reluctance is fear rooted in thinking about yourself. Think instead of how you can help your customer.

Nobody fears public speaking. What they fear is being judged.

Incomplete Transactions hold us back. Who should you follow through with? Who deserves an apology? Who needs to get an update from you?

Apology is drain cleaner. Say your apologies and get on with living.

How do you make the world better? Make yourself better!

Go shopping for great people to bring into your life.

Gratitude is nature's greatest magnet.

Always look for ways to make someone's life better today.

When problems appear look for growth not for shelter.

Music: The reason music is "the universal language" is because it transcends thought and goes directly to feeling.

Defensive behavior seldom protects you. Exploration of better ways is where your solutions lie.

Always seek Better. Better ways, better ideas, better solutions, better circumstances, better connections.

Want to know what to study about your business? Study the 11 Ps: Profit, Purpose, Principles, Product, Price, Places, Promotion, Processes, People, Payoffs and Performance.

"Optimism"

Think, Feel, Do
Think, Feel, Do
When you think you can, and when you think you can't
…you're right
It's a matter of mind not just a matter of might
To see it through your point of view is key
And you don't need to think the same as me
It seems completely plausible to say something's impossible
When you don't see how … you just assume - You Can't
But pessimism leads to less
The doubters don't clean up the mess
It takes no talent to tear others apart
The critic may be smart but has no heart.
Or you can choose to be among the Brave
The one who stands and faces every wave,
with certainty that peace and joy are near
if you only learn to look beyond your fear
Think, Feel, Do
If you think you could, you might
When you think you can, you're right
If you're pretty sure that somehow there's a way
Then you'll stay the course until you find
the success you hoped for in your mind
Hope sustains, Doubt refrains,
Dreams appear when we avoid the fear

What you think defines the way that you'll feel
If you doubt and criticize you'll make it real
But with Optimism you can make it so (Yes you can!)
You'll gain the strength to still get up and go
How you think is what you do
What you see can make things new
When you think you can or think you can't you're right
It's a matter of mind not just a matter of might
See what you want, feel the positive flow, think of the best
And Make It So!
Think, Feel, Do.

© Jim Cathcart 9-24-2014

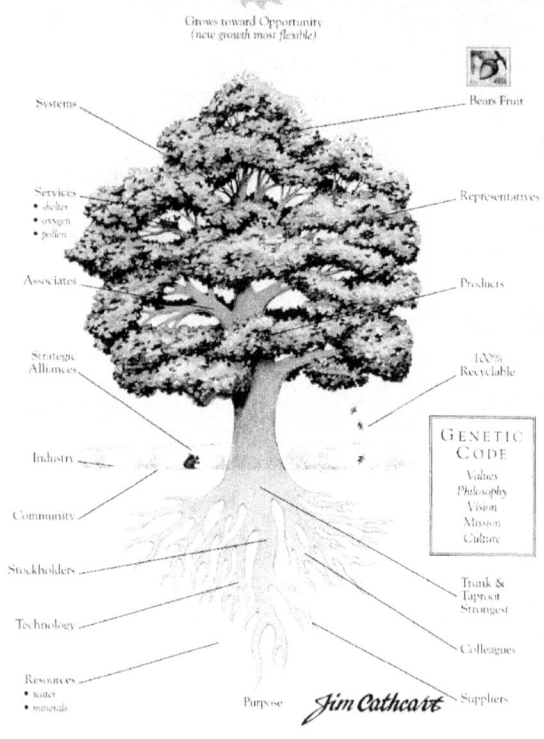

Business is the vehicle that a society uses to make its life better. A business is a living system, an organism, not a mechanism. Like a tree, it thrives by attaining the perfect interactive relationship with the ecosystem in which it lives.

Consider the qualities shared by a tree and a business. Both grow toward opportunity and send out roots to needed resources. Both follow their nature, and only their nature, (their genetic code) through predictable seasons and cycles, shedding unproductive parts and growing new parts as needed. Both are strengthened by adversity and bear fruit.

The Acorn Principle is: "The seeds of your future successes already live within you. So nurture your nature."

CONTACT INFO

Jim Cathcart
info@cathcart.com
Cathcart Institute LLC,
11712 Red Oak Valley Lane,
Austin, Texas 78732
1-805-777-3477

Main Website: *https://cathcart.com*
Meeting Link: *https://MeetLink.co/cathcart*
Digital Biz Card: *www.jimcathcart.com*
Linkedin: *https://www.linkedin.com/in/cathcartinstitute*
Amazon: *https://www.amazon.com/author/jimcathcart*
Facebook: *https://www.facebook.com/JimCathcart*
Instagram: *https://www.instagram.com/jimcathcart*
YouTube:
https://www.youtube.com/@The_Official_Jim_Cathcart
Wikipedia: *https://en.wikipedia.org/wiki/Jim_Cathcart*
X-Twitter: *https://twitter.com/jimcathcart*
Vimeo: *https://vimeo.com/jimcathcart*
TikTok: *https://www.tiktok.com/@jimcathcart88*
Scheduling Calendar: *http://bit.ly/callcathcart*

Winning Ways
Inspiring True Performance

Need a motivational speaker
or team building trainer?

Lisa Marie David

**Ziglar Legacy Speaker
Trainer & Coach**

Text or Call: 901-827-0115

inspiringtrueperformance.com

www.ingramcontent.com/pod-product-compliance
Lightning Source LLC
LaVergne TN
LVHW011901060526
838200LV00054B/4455